REALLY EASY JAZZIN' ABOUT
fun pieces for
DESCANT RECORDER

CONTENTS
Party popper! 3
Star-struck 4
Spiderman rock 6
Periwinkle waltz 8
Grandpa's old boiler 9
Funky doughnut 10
Dreaming 12
Sasha 14
Kingfisher 16
Bumble bee boogie 18
Willow 20
Let's jazz! 22

© 2005 by Faber Music Ltd
First published in 2005 by Faber Music Ltd
Bloomsbury House
74–77 Great Russell Street
London WC1B 3DA
Cover by Velladesign
Music processed by MusicSet 2000
Printed in England by Caligraving Ltd
All rights reserved

ISBN10: 0-571-52408-7
EAN13: 978-0-571-52408-2

PAM WEDGWOOD

Party popper!

Pam Wedgwood

Star-struck

Spiderman rock

Periwinkle waltz

Grandpa's old boiler

Funky doughnut

Dreaming

Party popper!

Pam Wedgwood

Happily ♩ = 132

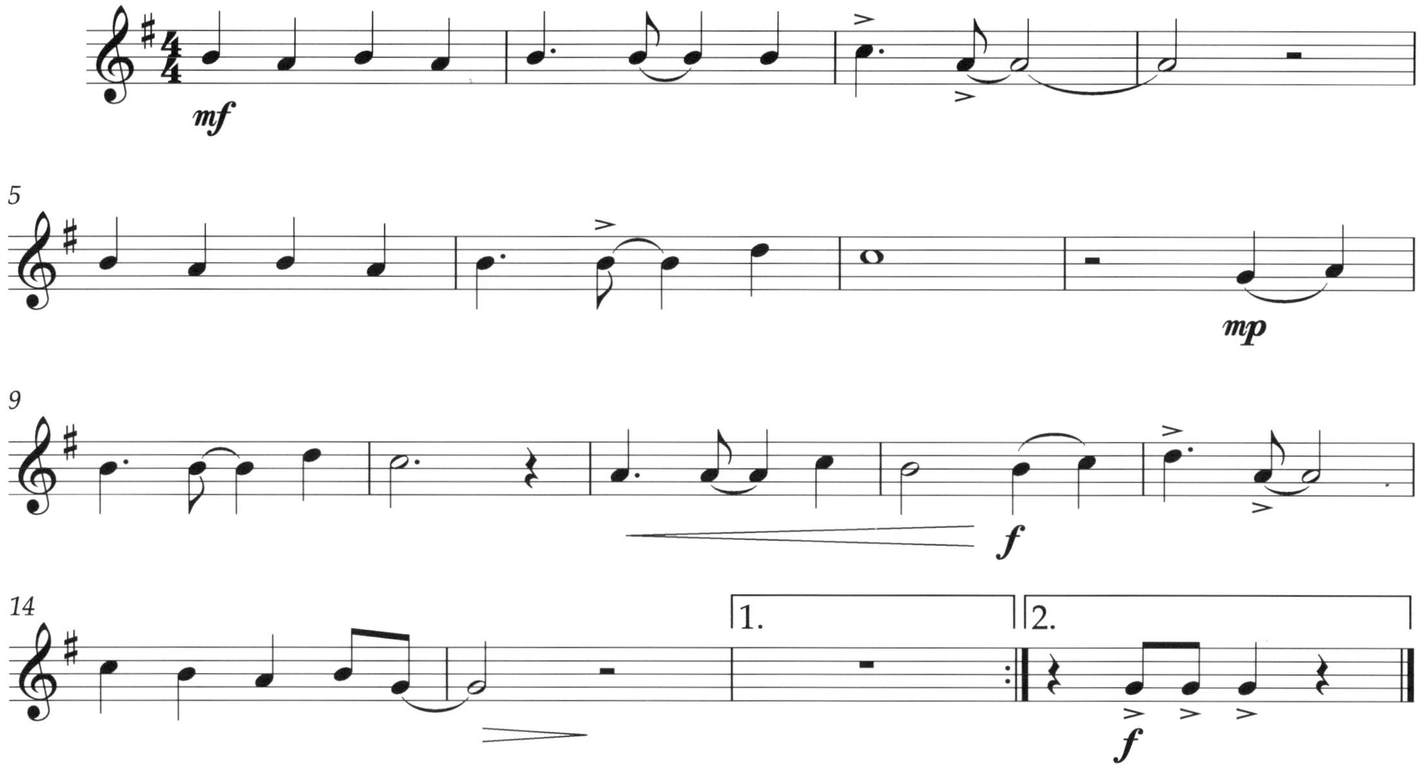

Star-struck

Mystical ♩ = 96

© 2005 by Faber Music Ltd This music is copyright. Photocopying is ILLEGAL and is THEFT.

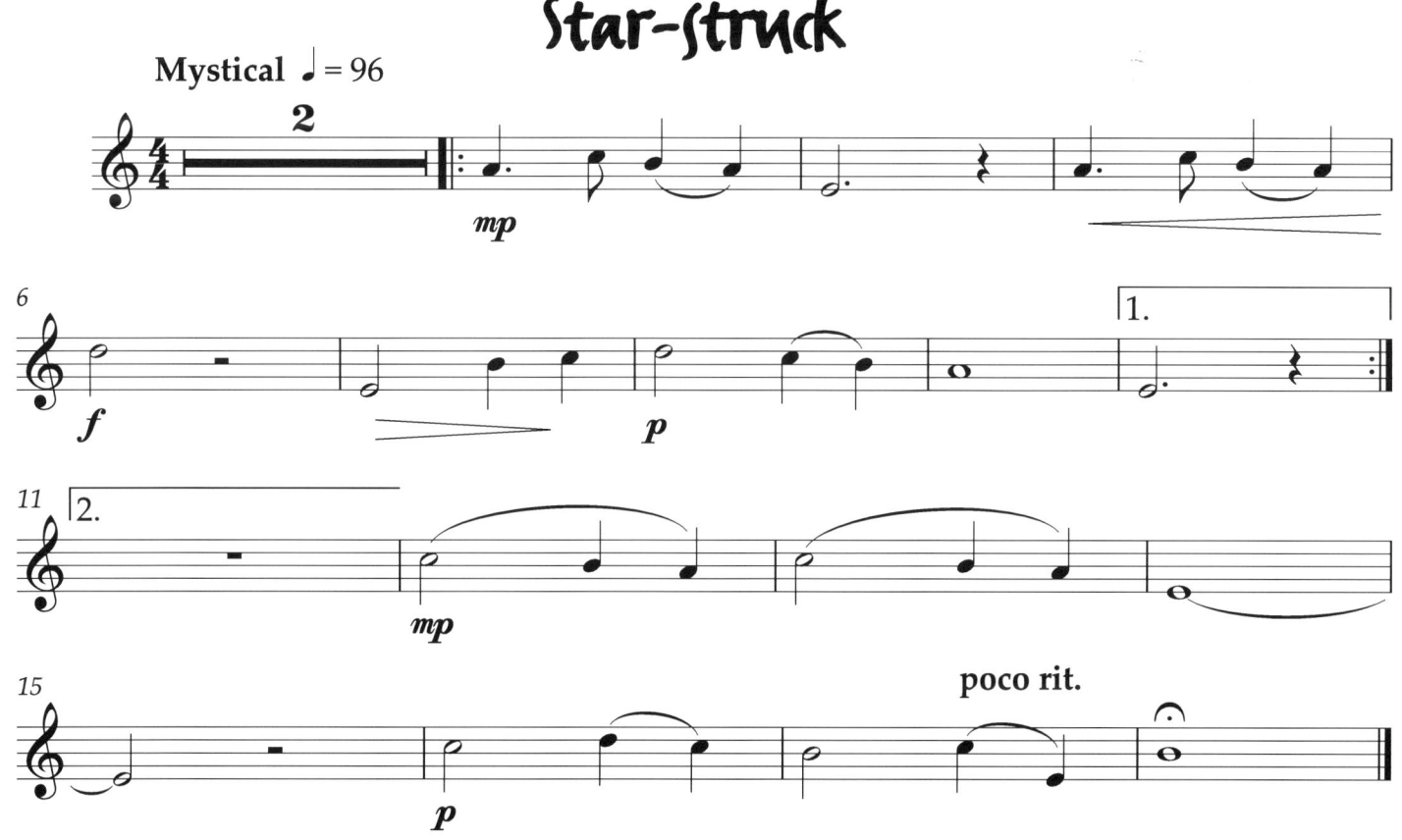

Spiderman rock

With a groovy beat ♩ = 120

Periwinkle waltz

In a carefree jazz waltz time ♩ = 120 (♪. ♬ = ♩ ♪ triplet 3)

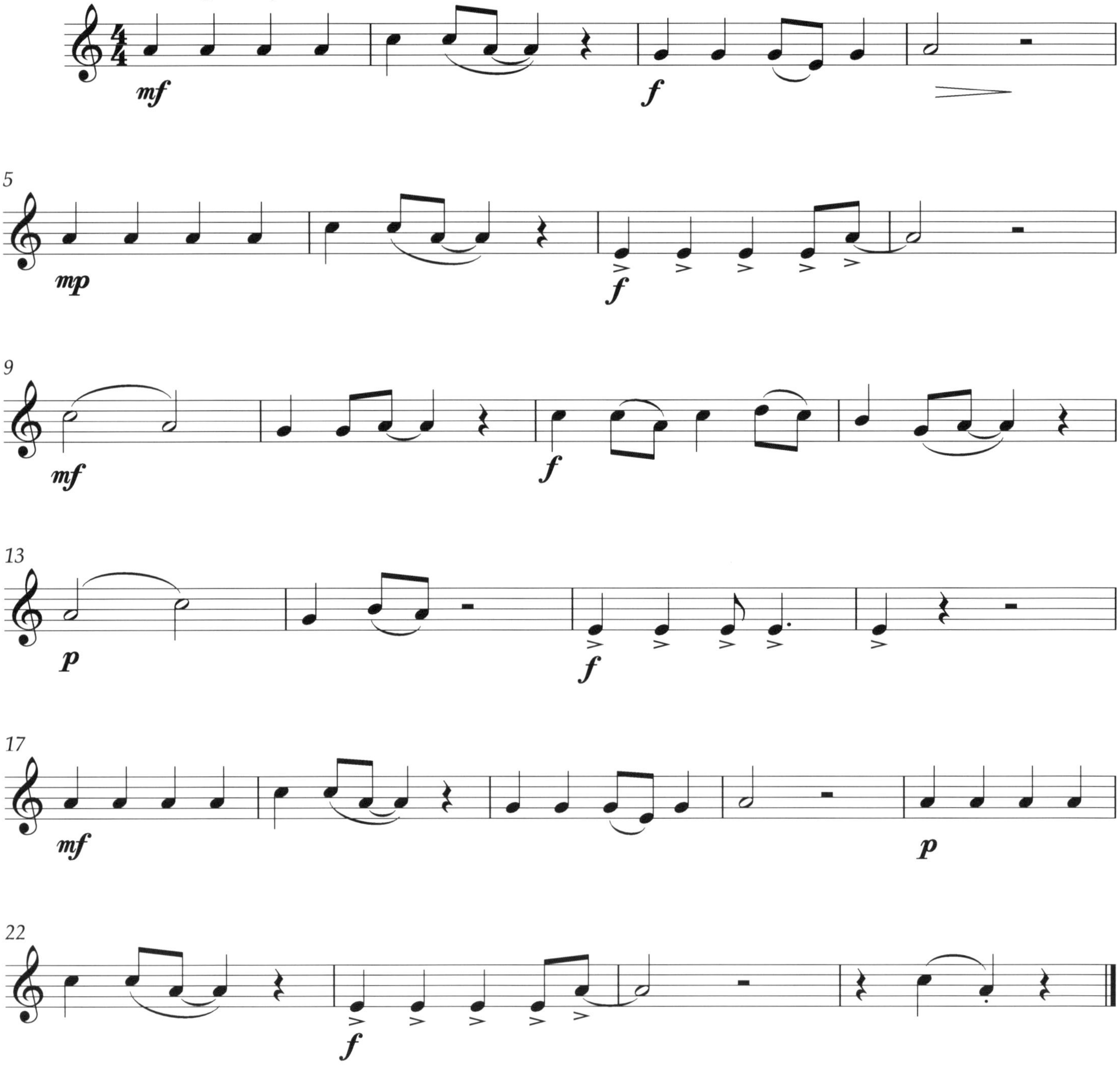

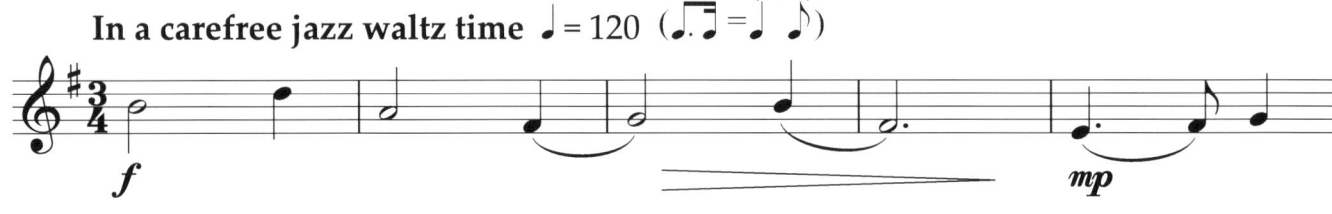

Grandpa's old boiler

Funky doughnut

Funky beat ♩ = 116

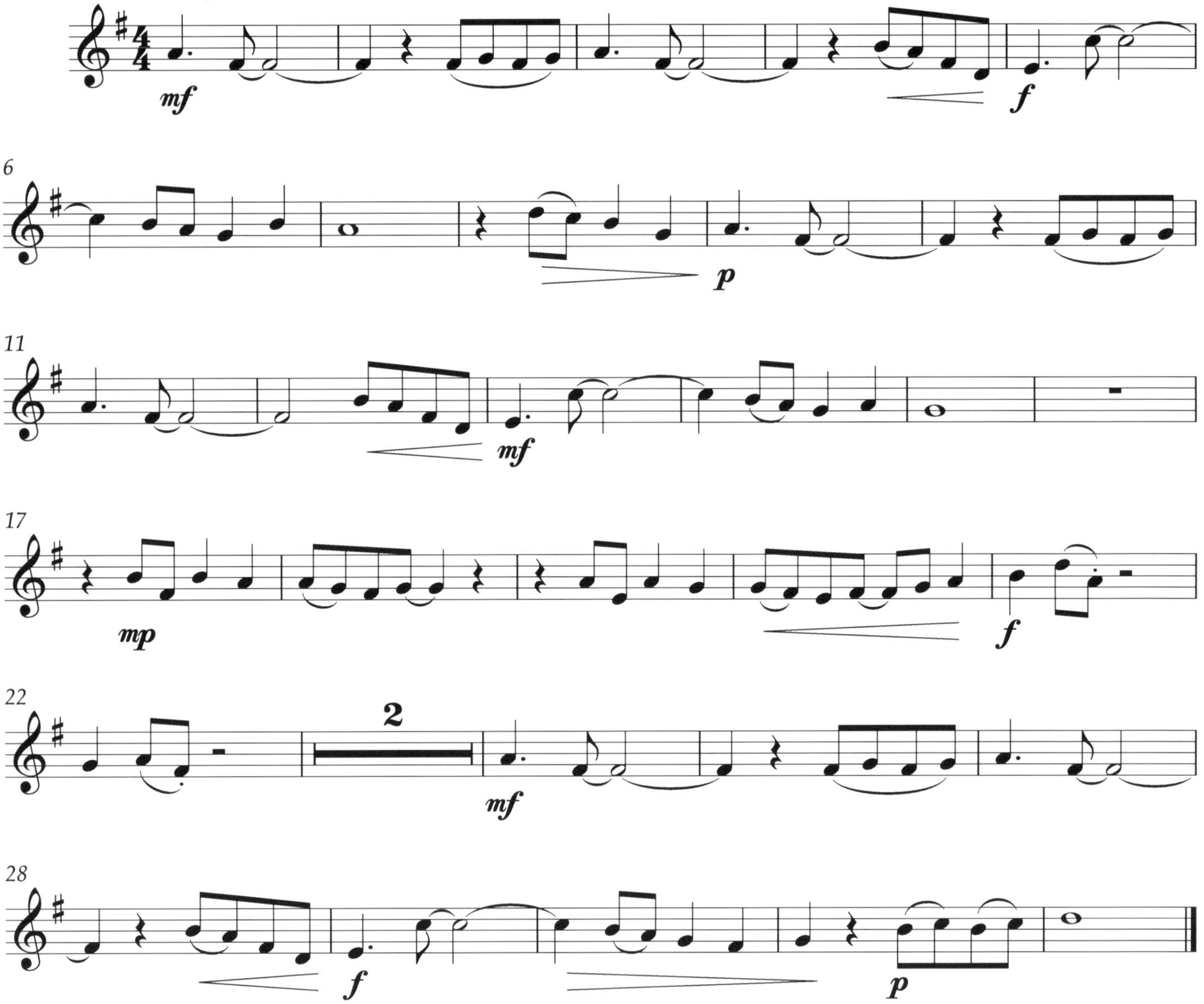

Dreaming

Dreamily ♩ = 100

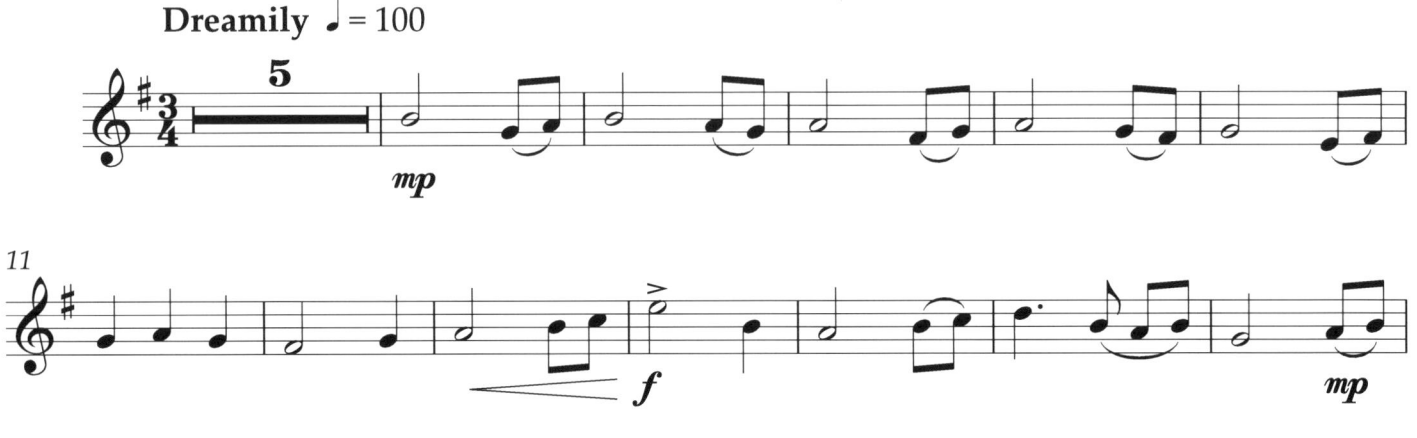

18
p
mp
25
f
32
rall.
p

Sasha

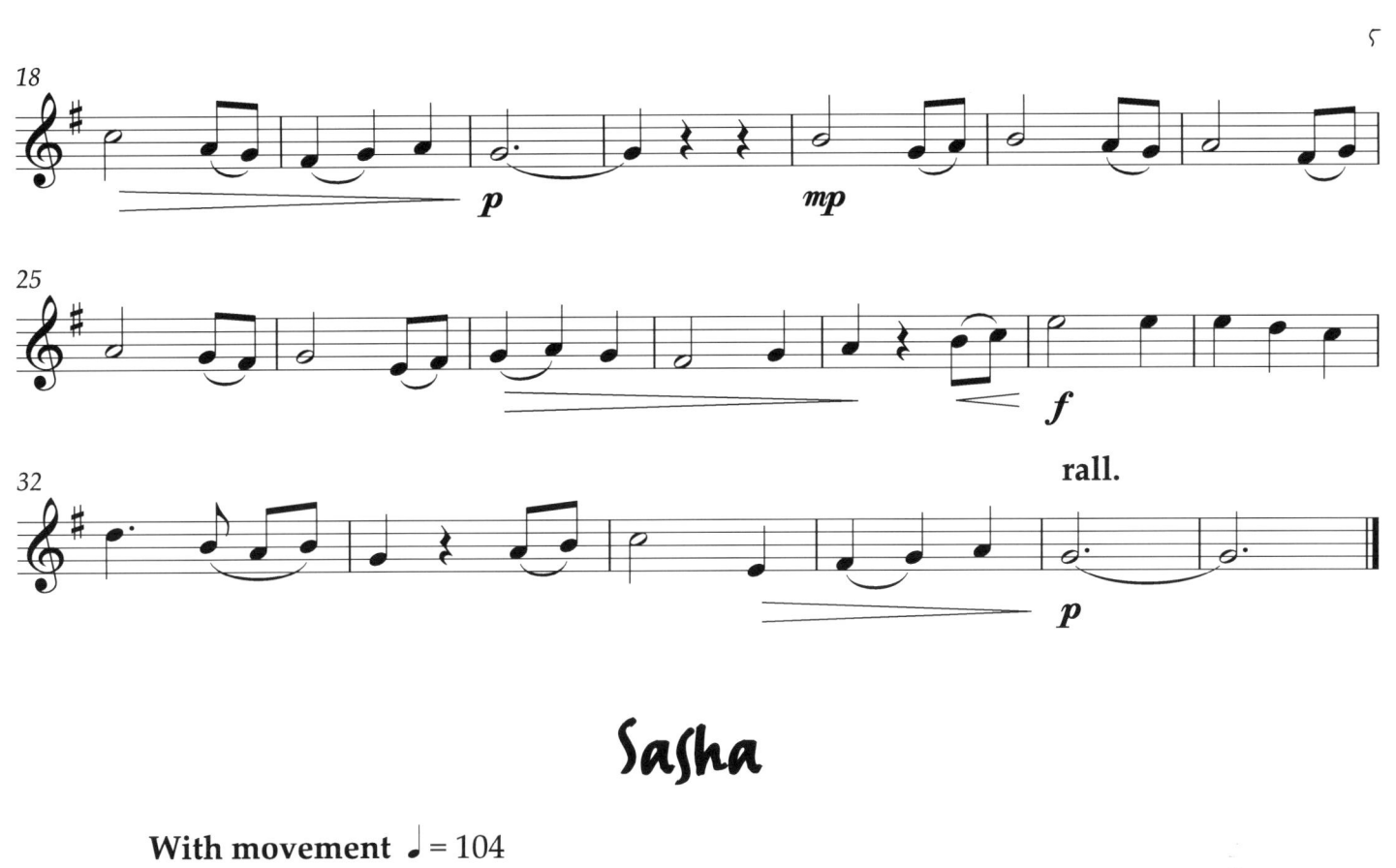

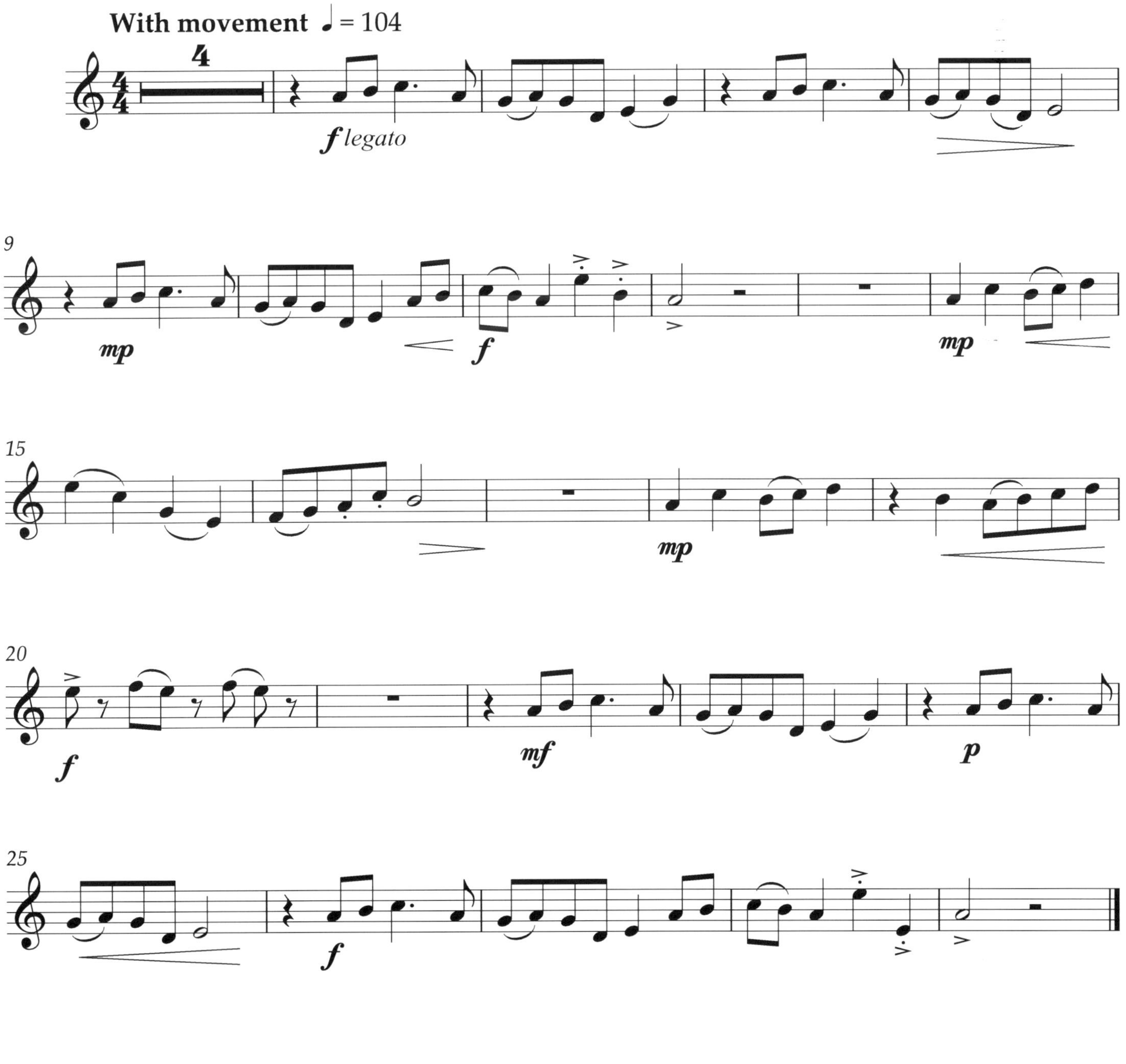
With movement ♩ = 104
4
f legato
9
mp
f
mp
15
mp
20
f
mf
p
25
f

Kingfisher

With gentle movement ♩. = 56

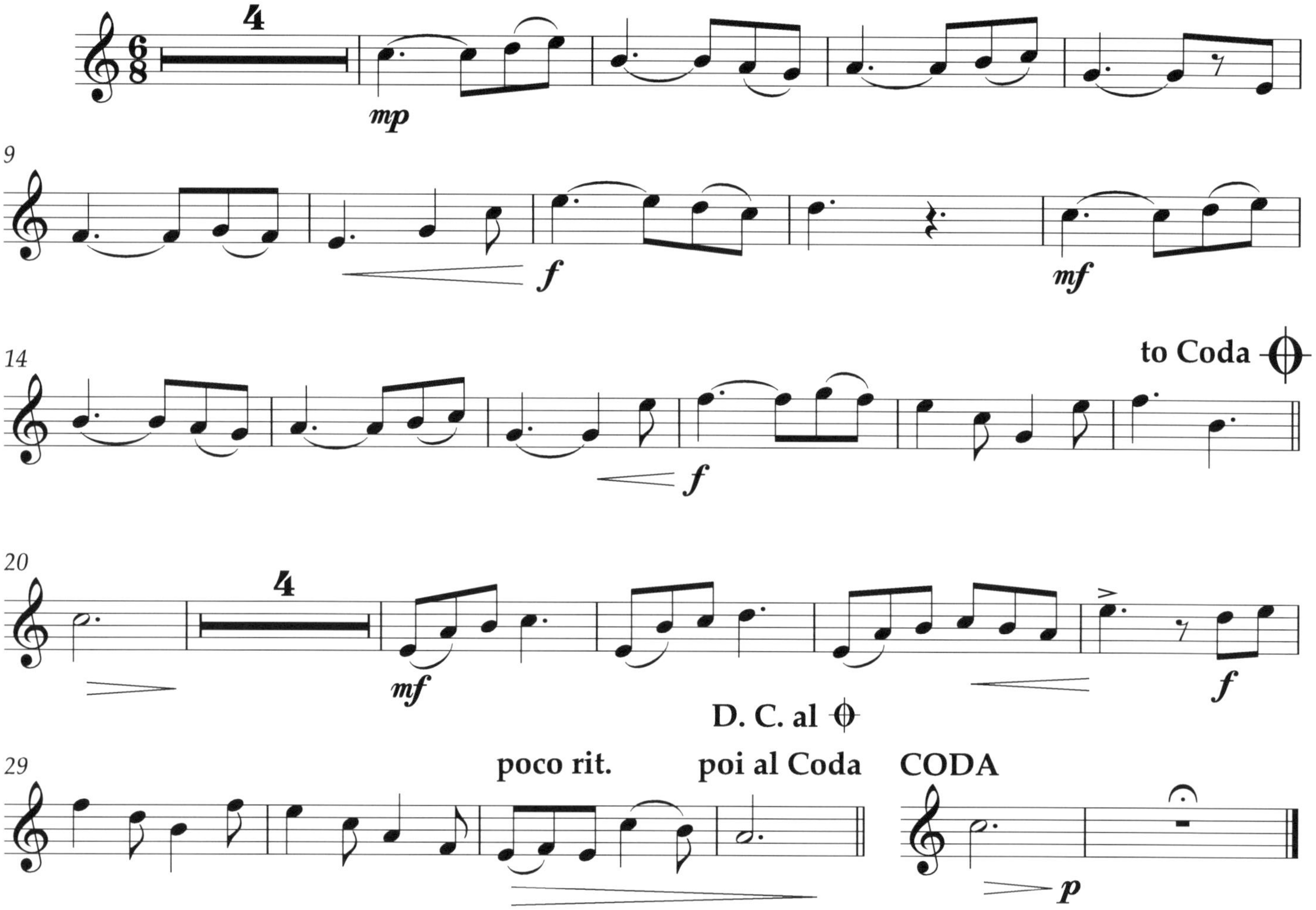

Bumble bee boogie

Buzzing! ♩ = 120

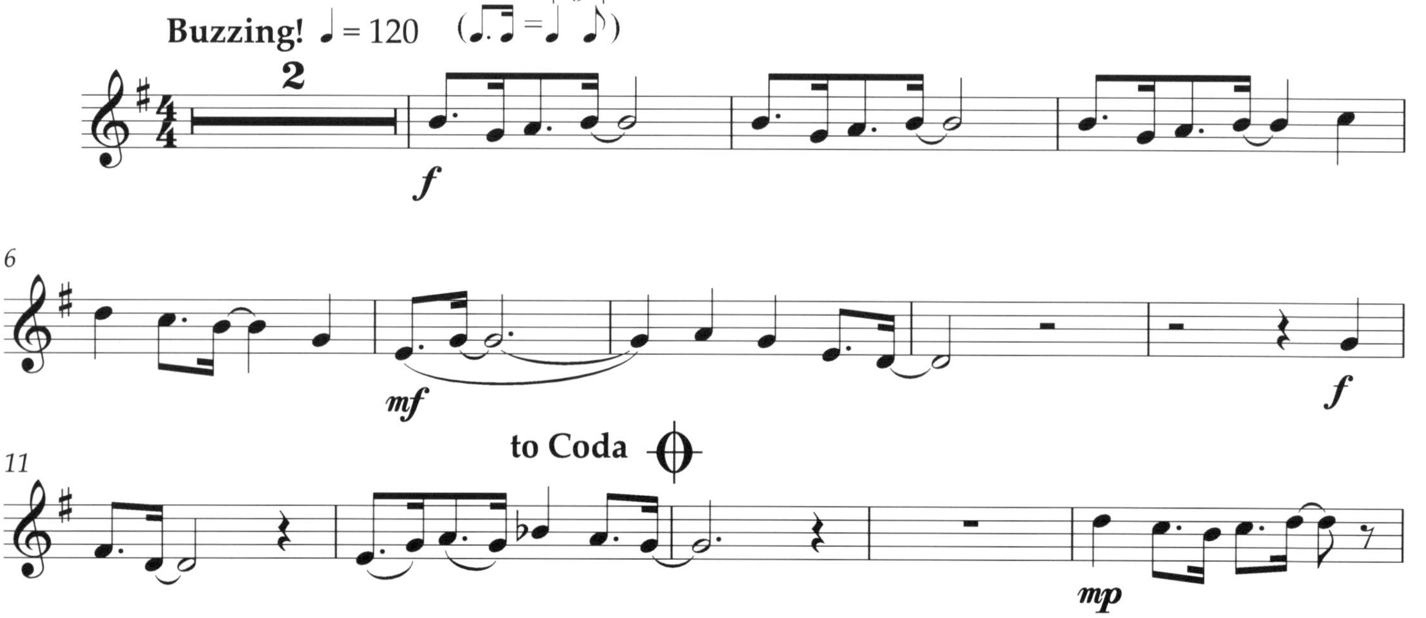

16
p
20
f
D. C. al ϕ
poi al Coda
24
CODA

Willow

In pop ballad style ♩ = 100
poco rit.
a tempo
4
p
mf
9
14
f
mp
19
p
f
24
mp
29
poco rit.
Slower
f
p

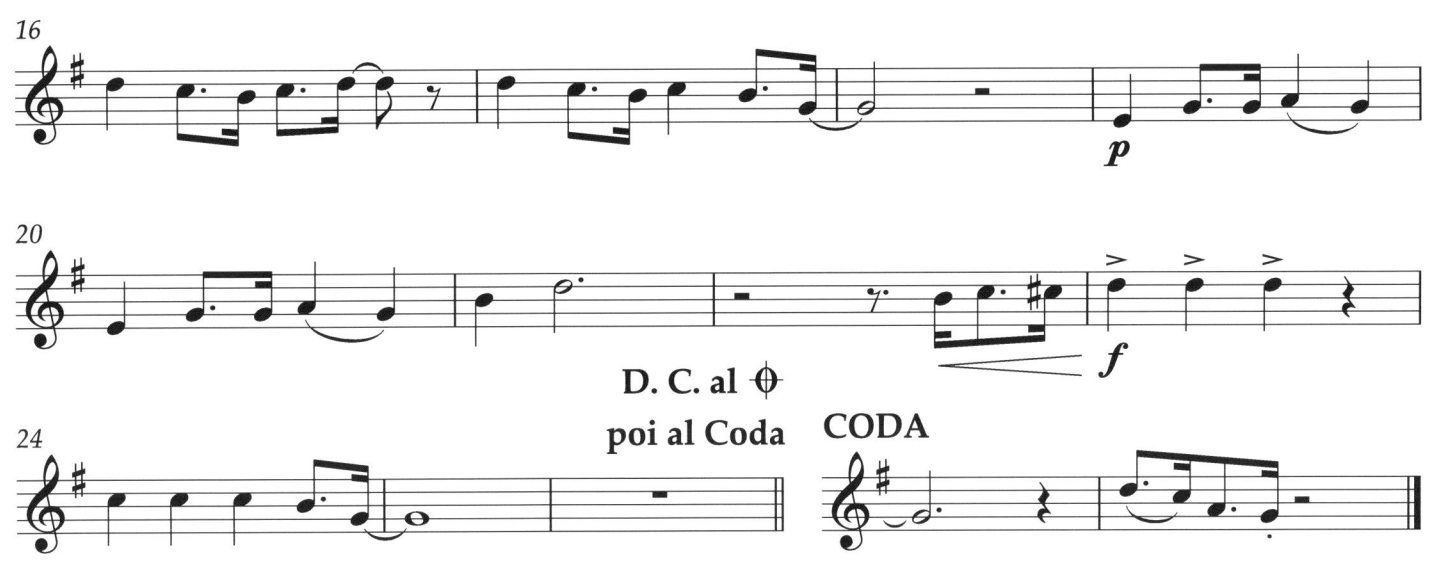

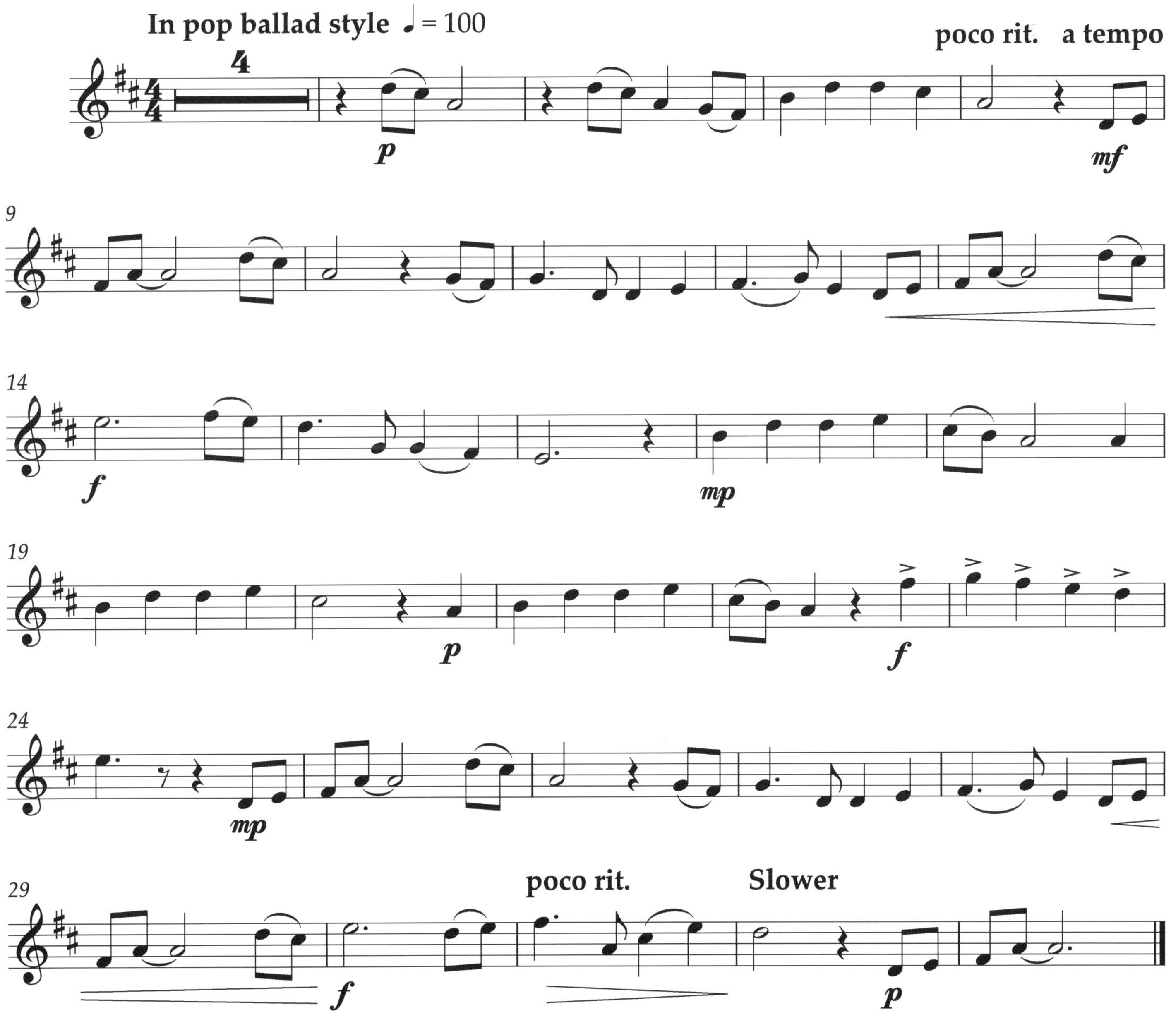

Let's jazz!

Latin beat ♩ = 108–116
Optional improvisation using suggested notes

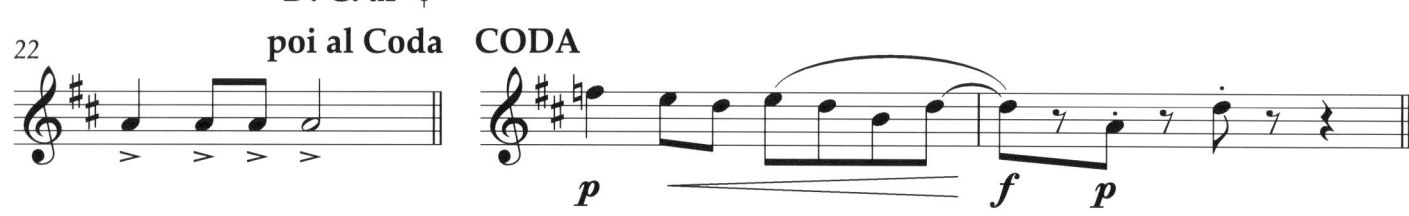

Sasha

With movement ♩= 104

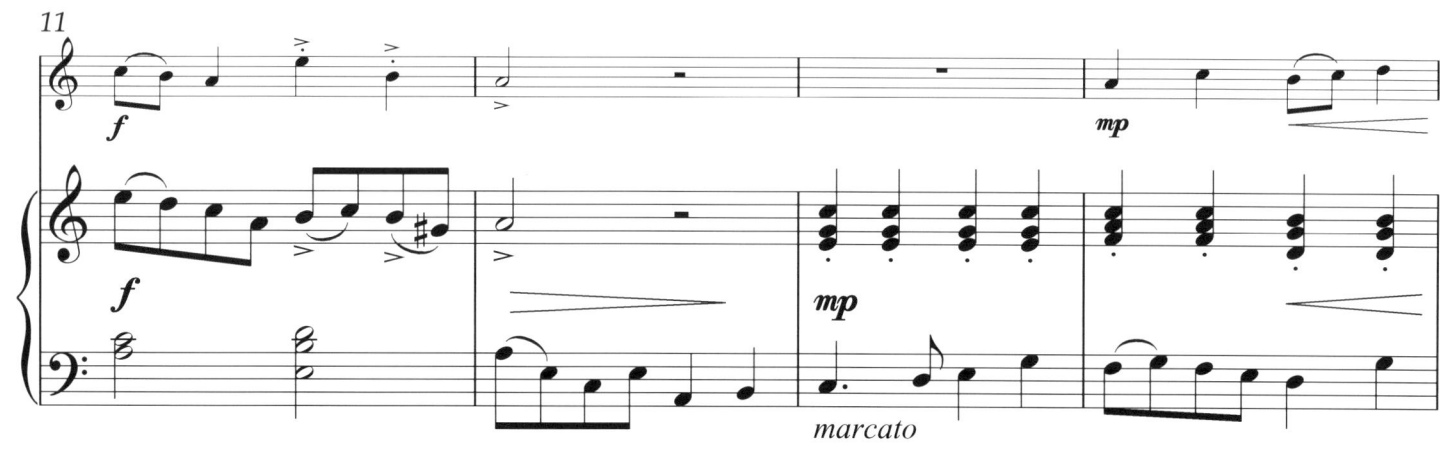

Kingfisher

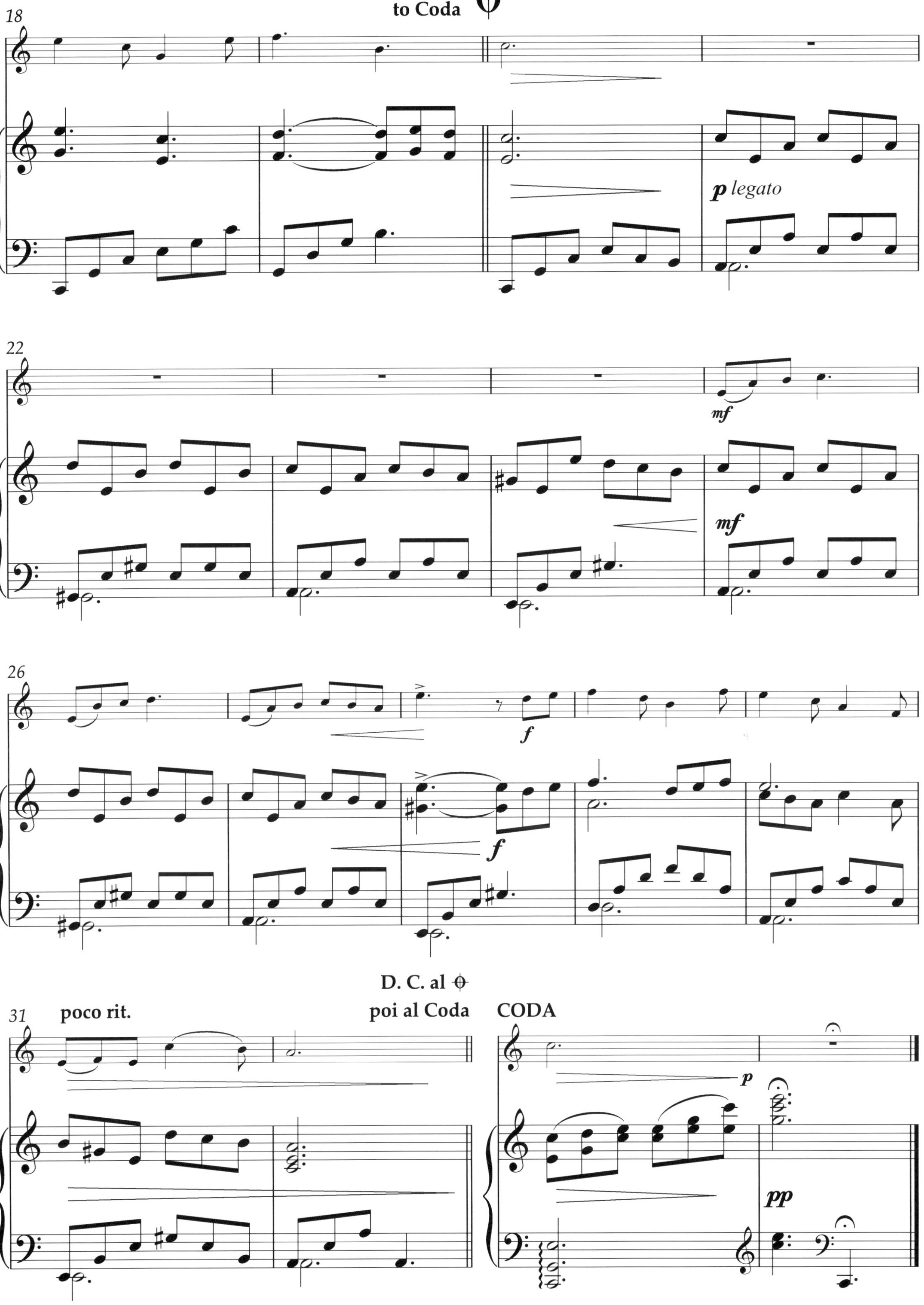
18
to Coda
p legato
22
mf
mf
26
f
f
31
poco rit.
D. C. al
poi al Coda
CODA
p
pp

Bumble bee boogie

Willow

Let's jazz!

The JAZZIN' ABOUT series
PAM WEDGWOOD

Jazzin' About. Trumpet	ISBN 0-571-51039-6
Jazzin' About. Trombone	ISBN 0-571-56943-9
Jazzin' About. Alto Saxophone	ISBN 0-571-51054-X
Jazzin' About. Piano	ISBN 0-571-51105-8
Jazzin' About. Clarinet	ISBN 0-571-51273-9
Jazzin' About. Flute	ISBN 0-571-51275-5
Jazzin' About. Violin	ISBN 0-571-51315-8
Jazzin' About. Cello	ISBN 0-571-51316-6
Jazzin' About. Piano duet	ISBN 0-571-51662-9
Green Jazzin' About. Piano	ISBN 0-571-51645-9
Easy Jazzin' About. Piano	ISBN 0-571-51337-9
Easy Jazzin' About. Piano duet	ISBN 0-571-51661-0
Easy Jazzin' About. Descant Recorder	ISBN 0-571-52329-3
More Jazzin' About. Piano	ISBN 0-571-51437-5
Christmas Jazzin' About. Piano duet	ISBN 0-571-51584-3
Christmas Jazzin' About. Clarinet	ISBN 0-571-51585-1
Christmas Jazzin' About. Flute	ISBN 0-571-51586-X
Christmas Jazzin' About. Violin	ISBN 0-571-51694-7
Christmas Jazzin' About. Cello	ISBN 0-571-51695-5
Christmas Jazzin' About. Trumpet	ISBN 0-571-51696-3
Really Easy Jazzin' About. Piano	ISBN 0-571-52089-8
Really Easy Jazzin' About. Flute	ISBN 0-571-52097-9
Really Easy Jazzin' About. Clarinet	ISBN 0-571-52098-7
Really Easy Jazzin' About. Oboe	ISBN 0-571-52124-X
Really Easy Jazzin' About. Bassoon	ISBN 0-571-52138-X
Really Easy Jazzin' About. Trombone	ISBN 0-571-52139-8
Really Easy Jazzin' About. Horn	ISBN 0-571-52172-X
Really Easy Jazzin' About. Alto Saxophone	ISBN 0-571-52197-5
Really Easy Jazzin' About. Trumpet	ISBN 0-571-52198-3
Really Easy Jazzin' About. Violin	ISBN 0-571-52201-7
Really Easy Jazzin' About. Recorder	ISBN 0-571-52408-7
Really Easy Jazzin' About Studies. Piano	ISBN 0-571-52422-2
Jazzin' About. Piano (with CD)	ISBN 0-571-53400-7
More Jazzin' About. Piano (with CD)	ISBN 0-571-53401-5
Easy Jazzin' About. Piano (with CD)	ISBN 0-571-53402-3
Really Easy Jazzin' About. Piano (with CD)	ISBN 0-571-53403-1
Christmas Jazzin' About. Piano (with CD)	ISBN 0-571-53404-X
Jazzin' About Styles. Piano (with CD)	ISBN 0-571-53405-8
Jazzin' About Standards. Piano (with CD)	ISBN 0-571-53406-6
Easy Jazzin' About Standards. Piano (with CD)	ISBN 0-571-53407-4

To buy Faber Music publications or to find out about the full range of titles available please contact your local music retailer or Faber Music sales enquiries:

Faber Music Ltd, Burnt Mill, Elizabeth Way, Harlow CM20 2HX
Tel: +44 (0) 1279 82 89 82   Fax: +44 (0) 1279 82 89 83
sales@fabermusic.com   fabermusic.com   fabermusicstore.com

This collection is gratefully dedicated to my dear friends and musical mentors, Co. Sligo flute player Tom Byrne (1920-2001) and Co. Leitrim fiddler Tom McCaffrey (1916-2006). With beaming smiles and a pat on the back they welcomed me into their families and their community, providing me with an immersion into the traditional music and culture of their homeland.

Tom McCaffrey and Tom Byrne in Cleveland, Ohio, 1975.

Acknowledgements and Credits

Many people helped me as I worked on this project. Some steered me toward important resources, some wrote books and issued tune collections, and some provided and maintained online bodies of information and music that were invaluable to me during my research. Others answered the call to review and comment upon my work as it evolved.

I offer my deepest gratitude to the scores of Irish musicians, living and passed away, who have shared their music with me so generously, person to person and through the medium of recorded sound.

I also wish to thank the following people and organizations: Archive.org, Kevin Atkins, Alain Barker, Bill Black, Breandán Breathnach, Jim Canary, John Chambers, Comhaltas Ceoltóirí Éireann, Paul Cranford, Bryan Kelso Crow, Paul de Grae, Janis Deane, Anne Dodson, Brian Duggan, Neil Fleming, The Irish Traditional Music Archive, Cynthia Jaffe, Thomas Johnson, Jeremy Keith, Andrew Kuntz, Merridee LaMantia, Amber Lipman, Terry McGee, Brooks McKinney, Zach Moon, Tom Norm Morrison, Brian Murer, Alan Ng, Henrik Norbeck, Capt. Francis O'Neill, Professor Gearóid Ó hAllmhuráin of the School of Canadian Irish Studies, Concordia University, Montreal, Lillis Ó Laoire, Vallerio Pelliccioni, Ardal Powell, Laura Rediehs, Dragut Reis, Patrick Sky, Fintan Vallely, Mimi Vidaver-Davis, Chris Walshaw and Lawrence Washington.

Above all, I wish to thank Cindy Kallet for her unflagging support, enthusiasm and patience, and for countless hours spent exploring ideas with me and lovingly examining this work with me from every angle.

Photo Credits:
Dedication: Richard Carlin (photo of Tom Byrne and Tom McCaffrey)
Introduction: Rich Remsberg (Figures 1 and 2)
Chapter One: Shannon Zahnle (Figure 5)
Back cover: Shannon Zahnle

Illustrations of larks, curlews, magpies, blackbirds and feathers by Janet Lorence.

David Armstrong developed the Larsen font that is used in this book for ornamentation symbols.

Audio recorded and mastered by Grey Larsen at Grey Larsen Mastering, Bloomington, Indiana USA.

Introduction

It was a delightful challenge to craft this book and its recordings, a journey of several years. Simultaneously, I put together its companion, *150 Gems of Irish Music for Tin Whistle*.

I culled tunes from many sources, consulting notated collections, old and new, and listening to hundreds of recordings of revered musicians, both living and passed on. I learned many of these tunes directly from friends in Ireland and the US, and from the elders who graciously mentored me into traditional Irish music during my teens and twenties. Some of the tunes have soaked their way into me over the course of thousands of informal music sessions, without a conscious attempt on my part to learn them. Others are newfound favorites.

To me they are all gems, tunes that I love to play on the flute. While many are well-known, others, as far as I know, have not been widely played in recent years.

The standard, wooden Irish flute is in the key of D. Everything in this collection is presented with that flute, and the modern Boehm-system flute, in mind. All references to flutes refer to these standard-pitched flutes unless stated otherwise. An exception to this is found in the Appendix, which addresses the issue of how to play certain tunes on Irish flutes built in keys other than D.

While most flute players who devote themselves to Irish traditional music prefer to play the wooden Irish flute, some prefer the Boehm-system instrument and become highly accomplished in playing Irish music upon it. For more, see "The Irish Flute and the Modern Flute" on p. 7.

This collection seeks to serve several purposes:

- To provide 94 tunes that fit the flute like a glove, that match its range, that favor its natural capabilities and steer clear of its limitations (Section One).
- To provide 28 tunes of non-wind origin (Section Two). These tunes keep to the Irish flute's natural scale but challenge players to accommodate certain characteristics of the non-wind instruments, such as their broader range and their versatility in the embellishment of C and C♯.
- To provide 28 tunes that require the use of keys on the Irish flute (Section Three). These tunes use one or more of the four pitches not found in the tunes of the two categories above: E♭, F♮, G♯ and B♭.
- To illuminate the tune transcriptions with suggested ornamentation and breathing places.
- To provide information on ornamentation, breathing, phrasing, modes and notation.
- To encourage learning by ear. The recordings of each tune make the suggested ornamentation and breathing options audible, and contain many facets of the music that cannot be written down.
- To introduce the idea of playing some Irish tunes, in their customary pitch and scale, on flutes that are made in keys other than D. Eight examples are given in the Appendix.

Section One: Flute-Friendly Tunes

These 94 tunes are utterly natural to the flute. They fall within the comfortable octave-plus-a-sixth range of the Irish flute and contain only the notes that are easily played by completely covering and uncovering its six finger holes: D, E, F♯, G, A, B, C♮ and C♯. The notes that most naturally invite ornamentation in these tunes are the ones that Irish flute players can embellish with variety and ease. For more on what makes a tune flute-friendly, see "Flute-Friendly Tunes" on p. 47.

Section Two: Tunes of Non-Wind Origin

I believe these 28 tunes originated with players of non-wind instruments such as fiddle, accordion, concertina, tenor banjo and harp. Most have notes that fall below the range of the standard Irish flute and require the player to make creative adjustments to the melody. Some include sequences of notes that may be more natural to a fiddle or accordion than they are to a flute. Some invite ornamentation on C and C♯, notes which are not as readily ornamented on the flute as on other instruments, notes which invite the flute player to employ finger and breath vibrato, shadings of pitch, tone and loudness, and melodic variation. Yet these tunes, like those in Section One, contain only the notes that are easily played by completely covering and uncovering the Irish flute's six finger holes: D, E, F♯, G, A, B, C♮ and C♯. For more about this class of tunes, see "Tunes of Non-Wind Origin" on p. 83.

SECTION THREE: TUNES REQUIRING THE USE OF KEYS

The remaining 28 tunes employ one or more of the four pitches that fall outside the natural scale of the Irish, or simple-system wooden flute: E♭, F♮, G♯ and B♭.

For players of wooden Irish flutes, these tunes call for the use of one or more metal keys. When these tunes come up in sessions, I see many flute players sitting them out while the fiddlers, accordion players, and others play on. If you have a keyed flute, why not use your instrument's chromatic capabilities, learn these tunes, and join in the fun? I hope this collection will encourage many players to do exactly that. For more information on this class of tunes, see "Tunes Requiring the Use of Keys" on p. 99.

Some of these tunes can also be played on keyless flutes that are built in keys other than D. For more on this, see the next two paragraphs.

APPENDIX: PLAYING TUNES ON NON-D FLUTES

Some tin whistle players keep a C whistle handy for playing tunes that contain F♮ and/or B♭, and many players collect whistles in other keys as well. Players of keyless Irish flutes, however, don't usually carry extra flutes around with them. More often they look forward to a time when they can upgrade to a keyed D instrument in order to play tunes that venture beyond the eight flute-friendly pitches (i.e., D, E, F♯, G, A, B, C♮ and C♯).

Nevertheless, you may enjoy exploring the various uses of non-D flutes. In the Appendix (pp. 112-123) I present eight tunes that can be played very well, at their *standard* pitch level, on keyless flutes in C, A and G. These same eight tunes are presented for D flute in earlier sections of this book. Playing such tunes on a non-D flute can result in very different tonal colors, unexpected ornamentation options, and the ability to play notes, in their customary register, that fall below the range of the D flute. On CD #2, you may compare the sounds of these eight tunes being played both on a D flute and on a flute in low C, low A or high G.